# THE JOY OF THE NEARLY OLD

# Other Books by Rosalind Brackenbury

## Novels

*Becoming George Sand* (Houghton Mifflin Harcourt)
*The House in Morocco* (Toby Press)
*Windstorm and Flood* (Daniel & Daniel)
*Seas Outside the Reef* (Daniel & Daniel)
*The Circus at the End of the World* (Daniel & Daniel)
*Crossing the Water* (Harvester Press, UK)
*Sense and Sensuality* (Harvester Press, UK & Taplinger, New York)
*A Superstitious Age* (Harvester Press)
*The Woman in the Tower* (Harvester)
*Into Egypt* (Macmillan UK)
*A Virtual Image* (Macmillan UK)
*A Day to Remember to Forget* (Macmillan UK & Houghton
Mifflin, New York)

## Poetry

*Yellow Swing* (Daniel & Daniel)
*Jaune Balancoire* (Les Editions de l'Amandier, Paris—French/English)
*The Beautiful Routes of the West* (Daniel & Daniel)
*Coming Home the Long Way Round the Mountain* (Taxus, UK)
*Making for the Secret Places* (Taxus, UK)
*Telling Each Other It Is Possible* (Taxus, UK)

## Short Stories

*Between Man and Woman Keys* (Daniel & Daniel)

# THE JOY OF THE NEARLY OLD

## Rosalind Brackenbury

Hanging Loose Press
Brooklyn, New York

Published by Hanging Loose Press, 231 Wyckoff Street, Brooklyn, New York, 11217. All Rights Reserved. No part of this book may be reproduced without the publisher's written permission, except for brief quotations in reviews.

www.hangingloosepress.com
Printed in the United States of America
10 9 8 7 6 5 4 3 2 1

Hanging Loose Press thanks the Literature Program of the New York State Council on the Arts for a grant in support of the publication of this book.

Cover art by Lincoln Perry: From a series entitled *Six Degrees*, 16" x 12", oil on Masonite

Cover design by Marie Carter

"Oasis", "A Man and a Woman and a Blackbird" "New York with D." and "Christmas Eve, Hidden Beach, Key West" have been published in French by *Le Scriptorium*, Marseille.

"The Blue Line" and "Ferry across the James River" were published in *Hanging Loose* 95. "Ashes" and "Goodbye" were in *Hanging Loose* 97.

"On Reading Antoine Emaz" was published by Barbara Dordi in the *French Literary Review* no. 14.

Library of Congress Cataloging-in-Publication Data available on request.

ISBN: 978-1-934909-25-6

# Table of Contents

IV.

V.

I.

# THE JOY OF THE NEARLY OLD

*on reading Mahmoud Darwish*

A poet who died
still loving it all, a poet
my age exactly, who died this year
on a table in a hospital in Texas
while they were jump-starting
his heart;

he said in the end that poetry
changes nothing in the world,
only poetry. But poetry, he told me,
is everything: your country,
your loves, your coffee cup,
the color of almond blossom,
the indelible touch of a lover,
the sky at the end of your street.
And then his heart gave out,
that tender muscle: it was poetry,
needed a lighter touch.

He said all sleepers are babies,
in our sleep we become young again.
I watch you sleep, then ardent upon the stairs,
going down fast like a young man,
carrying your fragile heart
like a blown rose.

The world can't see us.
We are too old to be noticed:
nobody watches us pass.
The nearly old live cloaked in privacy.

A man and woman old enough to be
grandparents. A poet who died
brokenhearted and joyful.

Alone again in a corner of a café,
invisible, crazy with joy.  Oh, the taste
of coffee!  The sunlight
of this morning, this one day,
Sunday, when the dancers are all
out in the street;

what can I say but that it's huge,
the joy of the nearly old.

## Love Lines

If the trackways of lips,
hands, bodies, trajectories drawn
by decades of desire, were visible,
we would all walk
striped as zebras,

spotted as leopards
blending into jungle shades
wearing our skins as charts
our loves have drawn on us

highways
and small pathways of adventurous
touch, crossroads, meeting places
where our different lovers
have blazed their trails

like dark maps marked
with clusters of electricity
the world at night photographed
from space

we would go illuminated
as Christmas trees, bearing
cross fires of lightning strikes,
star-burst scars of the great
conflagrations

## Seal Skin

Solid in your filled skin, hair wet,
lips smiling in the dark,
your hand in mine, calloused from the tools you use;
your heart beating its own unsteady secret,
you know what to do:
it is in you, the sea and its messages,
trappings of the ocean,
a wrecked hull and a stolen oar:
I see you leave, your trades at your belt,
a man going back to sea after years on land.

It's an old story, the salt rough air and gentle turbulence,
the urge of distance and the slower tread,
leaving after these land years,
these closets, bedcovers,
wrappings for the soul.
Packed away still
above us in the black attic:
the old tied parcel of furred skin
which one of us, one day,
will wear, riding the tide right out.

# THE SPACE BETWEEN YEARS

Runs deep like a canyon,
a corridor of dreams;
waking, I wonder
who called me.

Darkness comes ragged and early,
the days are bright and full.
Nobody knows what day
it is, what time.

We eat leftovers
and wonder what new thing
will shock us alive.

In the space between years,
oranges in a white bowl,
black walnuts in a basket,
letters on the table,
flowers, red and white
in a jug.

Tablecloths and sheets, washed,
fly out like sails upon the line.

In the space between years,
tea from thin china:
my friend talks of Beijing, Shanghai,
the vanished alleyways,
the new high rises.
The white orchid by the pool
blooms, the Christmas cactus
sprouts its rosy flowers.

Hot bread
burns our fingers.
The tea is green, smells of meadows,
I say, she says it smells of tea.
Across the pool, a finger of wind
draws the water taut.
Her cousin was in the movie,
*The Red Violin.* In my cup
a crumb swells and sinks

in these days passing like water.

# A MAN AND A WOMAN AND A BLACKBIRD

*after Wallace Stevens*

The blackbird in the elder
beside the honeysuckle
above the hollyhocks
on a quiet afternoon,
early June, in a courtyard
where nobody comes
on Saturday,

where we speak again of
love, life, death,
the huge uncertainties,
and hear the blackbird sing.

It's so much easier now,
not being young and in a hurry.
Nobody waits, nobody notices,
our time is our own.
It takes a lifetime to get here.

You say, he is singing to us,
he knows someone is listening;
and I wonder, is the world tuned
this way, so that for every note
of song there is a listener,
sometimes two.

## SEPTEMBER FOOD

This afternoon when we leave the bed unmade
and he runs downstairs smiling,
I dress and go out into the street;
the sky is soft and narrow as a scarf,
a hint of rain to come.

I walk among market stalls and choose
the foods of this season, mushrooms
from heaps on the barrows,
figs full of their grainy explosions,
their skin fragile as our own;
small black muscat grapes
still dusty with sun;

then a brown bag full
of damp knuckled walnuts
up from the country, thick and
hard to crack open for their still
elastic milky meat.

Difficult foods, that taste
of earth and smoke,

I want a feast of them,
these foods of autumn,
on a cool grey Tuesday, September,
when we have loved each other

so thoroughly, to find
the continued taste and smell
of what's not easy: the hidden
nut harvest,  frilled
chanterelles,

all that grows wild and sudden
and surprises us.

# THE STORY

*after Robert Bly's "The Threshers"*

There's no use whining over the way things are
The old habits hang on us like worn clothes
And the way to change is hard.

Have we thanked each other for our part in this?
Have we blessed the winds for blowing us here?
Have we thanked geography for coincidence?

It would be good to admit life is never perfect
And recite the litanies of gratitude
But it's probably best to go on hugging in the morning.

Let's just agree that we're different
And that we have to choose our own travel plans
And figure out some way to meet as strangers.

We can still delight each other meeting on the street
And we can still talk about that original café
But it will be hard to stop reading aloud each night.

We know that most stories don't have happy endings
And that ours is being made up as we go along
And the key's always under the conch shell on the porch.

# BALANCE

Sometimes I can stand on one leg.
Sometimes I am happy to sleep alone.

Other times I teeter and fall,
Wobble, weep. Reach out
and shudder to find him gone.

The cool expanse of emptiness.
At least neither of us died,
at least it was chosen.

But what did I choose and
what chose me? Is something
behind the door that I have not seen?

I take my pose. Breathe. Balance.
Today I can do it. An image forms,
a story I have invented

to cheat death by going separate ways
so we can't be found easily
idling in each others' arms.

One will go this way, the other that.
One by sea, the other by land.
One on the low road, one on the high.

It won't find us; we'll be out there,
armed, alert, up for it.

## ON THE SHORES OF THE CHESAPEAKE

He found a horseshoe crab's shell,
I found a turtle's rib.
He found a deer's straight
femur, a sturgeon's teeth,
I found an oyster's platter
gleaming silver,
a bland clam.

I rolled up my pants,
he took off his shirt;
we went barefoot
crazy with pleasure
in the slip of sand,
our winter feet
shoe-shucked, our faces
turned to the low sun.

All around us the crabs
who had come out to dance
their airy quicksteps
in dry sand, rushed back
into their holes,
waited for us to leave.

# FERRY ACROSS THE JAMES RIVER

It's not a dream; but the memory
of one afternoon, late, when the sun
lowered over the shore we'd left
and the water was carved by the bow wave
in a deep almost colorless curve;
you stood at the stern of the ferry
and I came to find you, I knew
you'd be there wearing your jacket,
cap and gloves; and above you
the gulls, their bellies lit by the low sun
from underneath, hundreds of them
following the wake. The deck was iron,
the cars packed close, small children
hung on parents' hands; it was cold,
or beginning to be cold; the bank
we'd left behind was far, we were
midstream and turning before the current
and I came to you and we kissed in that
burnished end of afternoon.
It wasn't a dream, but now I see this
again and again, our brief life
together between two banks:
back there the quiet beach
where we searched for scallop shells
and driftwood to carry home,
before us, soon, the landing place
and above us the gulls, their feathers
fiery as angels'.

II.

# Oasis

Today, it's a cool hotel
where someone hands my friend and me
champagne in tall glasses
midafternoon. Mosaic
edges the pool.
Among glossy palms
small fat gods ride
sculptured ostriches
to victory.

We take off our clothes
and sink into blue water.
Tall trees shut out
traffic and drunken cries,
we are protected.
It is the first of many oases
along the way.

Dusty, hurt by what
we are seeing, we come
again and again to the idea
of oasis. Calm, watered, green,
a poem can be oasis:
come into the green gardens,
sit by the waterfall.

Someone will bring us
towels and a tray, her loose heels
clattering on flagstones
as ripples shift to the deep end
and darkness collects
under the leaves.

## St. Malo, Solstice

All night the sea fumbles
at the locks of sleep.
The tide's insanely far out
last thing and early;

in between,
a black web drawn taut,
in the small hours, unseen.

Late evening,
midsummer, gulls scatter
their shadows still and rise
like the kites boys sail
before the wind

curved like boomerangs
their sideways parentheses.

the whole
huge enterprise of tide,
sand shining like water,
water like pewter

the sea's frill nearly
invisible, these huge gestations,
vast accomplishments.

At this edge you can spin
anything up
and see it fly: a year,
a life, a thought.

# NEW YORK WITH D.

Two azaleas in the back yard blaze,
one pink one orange
when the light comes in slant.

Our English voices clip along the street
amazed at everything; we are on our way.
The trees are very frail green, getting stronger
thicker every day. It's May.

So easy to love it all. The man in the basement
singing opera, or making it up,
strong coffee in the bottom of a cup.

O, look at the wisteria!
It lies in wait for me yearly,
this month of my birthday, hugs like a mother,
climbs here all ropes and knots.

Striding through the Park, we are young
still and have our sneakers on, our backpacks,
noses into the chill wind, a scatter

of cherry-petals and a Chinese bride
sinks like a collapsed umbrella in the grass;
the grooms are all in white with red nosegays.

Everyone is a New Yorker, even us.

## With J. in Nice

The blue mane of Chagall's little horse:
that yellow person stretching in his paradise;

all the color that lifts and moves us so,
we go almost crazy with it, could eat
the ice-cream facades,
pink dome of the hotel Negresco,

roll in the curve of Matisse's single wave.

Here in Nice we walk
gazing upward
to the blue cutouts of sky snipped

from white angles of walls
to bougainvillea toppling
from balconies, and down
to jacaranda, lavender, wisteria,

agapanthus, blues of the heart,
blues of the ways of love,
umbrella blue, striped blue,
shirt on the beach blue; then, cool

green glass of the hollowing wave
bursting as white.

All the palaces, the ochre, burnt sienna,
antique red, all the green shutters
cracked and aged with sun, all
the paint laid on, centuries of it.

Walking with you, a painter,
I want, not words, but this:

to lick it up on a brush tip,
spread it on: the way the sky spreads — look —
blue, after storm, at the street's end.

# The Handkerchief

On the far side
hidden from the day's
midsummer heat, a place
under willows.

Nobody comes.
My old friend lays down his handkerchief
on still-wet grass.
Invited, I sit on his small blue-edged
cotton square

Here at a curved sand beach
at the great river's edge,
we pause to hear the quiet movements
of its shallows.

Small, small the difference
between perfection and what is not,
all the difference there is:

when the world stills,
the centre holds;

the way the river flows
lapping most gently,
the way gnats fill the air,

the way he places
his handkerchief, the way I sit on it,
the way his hand,
dragonfly over water,
nearly skims mine.

# BEES

*for E. at the Institut Curie, Paris*

Outside the clinic, where they zap cancer
with radio waves and the people go in
tattooed to mark the site

and where you will emerge at six-thirty *pile!*
to meet me, wearing your turban, lipstick
and a good coat as if to a party,

there are bees in hollyhocks
in a wild garden, just a narrow strip
nobody needs or tends, between

the cancer clinic and the Ecole Normale Sup.
I pause to watch the bees
push their way wriggling in

to the deep frilled interiors
to fumble and sip at their hidden
source.  Even the closed flowers

hold a bee, I can see their dark
furred bodies as if through a pale curtain;
twenty bees or so, hollyhocks,

long grass, lilac and buddleia.
Waiting for you, watching the bees
(who are supposed to be in decline)

I catch the buzz and frisson
of their deep intent. You come out smiling, yes,
we'll get a cab, have dinner, laugh, drink wine.

# EATING THE FIG

*Isle-sur-la-Sorgue*

Figs grow close to the mill wheel
where river water drips,
cools us in the instant we pass.

The fig tree sucks up water
and gives back, green hands
against the varied skies of August.

The fresh hard balls
under the fig leaves in the garden,
those naked male babies
we gave birth to long ago:

a few days rain and they are
soft as the lovers'
of our middle age.

We touch them daily,
then it's time
to take the first ripe one down,
divide it on a white plate
and eat.

Skin splits
to a rosy grain,
a dense mouthful
packed for endless fruiting
of futures in this place

not yet sweet but perfect
on the tongue, old
as all beginnings.

## AT THE SUPER-U

Surely not in France?  Not
where market stalls spill lettuce, beans,
cherries, melon, even ten
different kinds of potato?
Where people ask you to taste
and choose your olive, your particular
aged cheese?

Yes, here. Adjust your vision
at the door of the freezing supermarket
slapped down in the midst of fields
where the harvester
only yesterday
cut its yellow canyons
under the wooded hill:

the Super-U.  Sunday morning
and cars fill the parking lot.
Everyone who might have been
called by a cracked bell to mass
or at least to finger warm tomatoes
in the market place, humming
Georges Brassens, soaking up
the sun, is here:

orange plastic baskets, meat
slabbed under cellophane, vegetables
ditto, pasta, underwear, champagne;
you can buy a petit café
and hear a man say to his son
as he rushes a little brother
with a plastic gun, "You are not
in America."

But he's wrong, we are all in America,
permanently in America, and we will down
our cleaned vegetables, our shined
fruit, five a day, not for pleasure,
not out of hunger or need,
but doing what we're told
in the Super-U, on Sunday, in France.

## Paris Sunday

I wake from afternoon sleep,
make tea in the small kitchen,
crumbs under my bare feet like sand.
Yellow curtains brush the floor,
the table is round, small, covered
by a striped cloth.  From here
I speak to my husband in America
where he is  beginning his day
and try to tell him
how couples danced in the square
and one was a boy in fishnets
and stilettos, another a man in white
with a ponytail, and how a woman
sang, and the bells rang like fountains,
the street was all cherries and apricots
and everyone, at the same time,
sat down to eat.

# VERT GALANT

There's still the willow
and a couple kissing there
and Henri IV on his horse
all set to ravish the Place
Dauphine where I had lunch
today at a table, with Sancerre;

the promise made fifty
years ago to my young self
sitting under the willow
gnawing my baguette,
my friend and I taking swigs
from the bottle of rough red.

The Pont des Arts is still
there, and the Seine flows
green and barges pass.
I sit on a green bench
and wonder, is it the same
willow fingering the water

and am I the same
girl in love with it all,
who said, one day she'd buy lunch
for herself in a Paris restaurant
not counting the cost
and has just done so?

## Opening the Hives

*Les Jardins du Luxembourg, May*

The bees have their hidden houses,
pitched-roof pagodas at the garden's
green centre, a bee village

roped off now with the warning
"Ouverture des Ruches"
so parents tiptoe children away — ssh,

and the bee-keepers, hatted, veiled,
gloved, dressed in white
like garden party guests

from another century, start
their antique deliberate moves;
smoke in a small plume rises

spreads in the still air.
The bees come out.
Are they angry, shocked, upset?

I can't tell. They carry
The world's survival.
Little furious gods, they must get

our whole attention.
Incarnate futures, winged prophets,
their language a sibilance

we will have to learn, their dervish
dance our own cells'
necessary swarming.

# Home

When he asked me in the Contrescarpe bar,
Where's home? I couldn't say.

At eighteen, Paris glimpsed at dawn
through a taxi window:
Scotland, for more than a decade.
At forty-nine, Key West.

Home, I think now, is the path I took
sixty years ago, and take today;
where last week I saw an adder in the sun,

where once I walked, a child
with a stick against snakes, looked out
for mines and bombs, touched nothing
at our grandmother's orders,

where I stand tonight at the road's end
to see the raw gleam of an autumn sunset;
where aged eleven my cousin and I stretched lines
for a bush telegraph;

where thirty years ago, my lover
jumped out of a downstairs window;
where there are too many stories to tell;

where the shape of the land is like
the backs of old sleeping animals
and cloud comes over the hill
like bonfire smoke.

III.

# Letters Home

It's cold.
Thick fog in Cambridge.  Leaves fall.
I'm in love.  We have a punt on the Cam.

I've been jilted, please send food.
Roast chicken, please, a cake.  Shortbread
would be great.  Please send
my evening dress, the long one,
when it's back from the cleaners,
I've been asked to a ball.

I have become a beatnik. It saves
laundry and decisions about what to
put on. I just wear black. I miss you.
Thanks for the parcel, we all
enjoyed the cake.

Three men said they were in love with me.
I don't go to lectures any more.
My supervisor in Kings flirts and smokes a pipe.
My European history tutor is pregnant.

Graham's in the cricket eleven,
Howie's on the basketball team,
Charlie ditched me for a girl from home.
They all have girls from home.

It's all going much too fast.
I bicycle everywhere.
I'm in love with everything.
I wish you could see it all,
I wish you could see me,
madly, furiously, bicycling, in love.

## SCHOOL, 1950S

Going upstairs was unimaginable.
It was a kingdom you could not enter
till at ten or so you were chosen
for geometry and Latin.

Two bulldogs sat at the bottom step
their ochre eyes fixed, rough jaws
whiskered and salivating,
Digby and James.

Ascending the stairs was serious,
the end of play.  We knew
the teachers slept up there,
had a bathroom, even undressed.

The normal temperature of a body,
my mother told me, shaking down the thermometer
is 98.4 degrees.  But this ascent
was fever, white-out, no return.

We went up one by one
to sit at proper desks,
mine beneath the cool forever gaze
of Vermeer's *Girl with a Pearl Earring*.

I had a fountain pen, leaking ink,
my third finger tattooed indigo.
We learned how Horatio held the bridge
and about the Ghost of Christmas Past,

we swore by the Nine Gods,
painted in water colors, staining our jam jars,

fought duels in the break.
Upstairs, you could not imagine

ever having been downstairs
where small children still drew rabbits
in colored chalk on the board,
peed their pants, cried to go home.

We had work to do. When
we had finished, we took copies
of the *National Geographic*
and looked for pictures of naked people.

Unlike Elizabeth Bishop,
I did not find them horrifying.
Between the *Girl with a Pearl Earring*
and the buttocks of Masai warriors,

upstairs, I fomented
nameless desire, way above
the normal temperature of humans,
writing and burning in secret, burning and writing.

# BEING ENGLISH IN KEY WEST

*for Sheridan*

We've started, wine in our glasses,
rolling back the years: Ibiza, Biba's,
the Portobello Road,
the slow stain of the fifties in retreat;

those changing rooms where
we stripped off old selves,
in the same remembered frenzy
pulling on the velvets of the new decade.

We must be the same age, you and I.
From that time's fog, landscape of weather
and wit that no American will ever
understand, we go back further

till I see your trotting fingers in midair
hear the clop of wooden hoofs on a piano top,
caught on the grainy fizzing screen
in the brown box of the earliest TV

and Muffin the Mule prances there
strings visible, head cocked; the puppeteer
chats, smiles, sings: it's Annette Mills
who sadly died of cancer though

they'd never use the word, teatime
in Muffinland. We grin, remembering,
and know our nomad transatlantic lives
and everything in between

sprung from that childhood place
where they drew curtains, sat us down,
clicked the brown knob to On,
and Muffin started dancing in the dark.

## SPLINTERS

First, she'd burn a needle in a match flame
so it turned bruised indigo
to probe the place, picking the brown end out,

then lower her face to my flat hand
to find the tip with tongue and lips
and bite it free.

This fierce surprising intimacy,
the press of teeth, harder than a kiss,
her warm breath in my palm

and afterwards,
just a sore red spot, as she showed,
calm as a magician,
the splinter pulled out whole.

Biting her way,
each time a small shock,
my mother pulled hurt cleanly
from my astonished flesh.

# HER LAST AFTERNOON

We whomped the borrowed wheelchair
over sills and out into the air.
August, and the trees were dark,
sky an unlikely blue.

In the hospital gardens,
a thrush, she immediately knew.
A lifted hand to say, hark.
Out here for an hour or two

we sat with her, she
high on the beauty
of this revolving world,
trees shifted their weights

breeze twirled seeds down
hinting at autumn.
Oh, how lovely. Her skin
smoothed, eyes opened

for a last view,
a last summer afternoon
as it turned out,
last touch of sun and air

last green, last blue.
How can we imagine this
for another? Our mother at
eighty-nine, knowing,

not knowing; we had no idea,
death coming that night
and she, ecstatic
at just the way things were.

## GOODBYE

Yesterday, my father's birthday.
Born in that young century,
upon the cusp of Pisces and Aquarius,
he would have been 103.

Nobody lives to 103 except for rare old women
grinning in nursing homes or men
who live off yogurt in the Caucasus
booted and toothless, with fierce eyebrows and lost eyes.

He quit at eighty-six
angry with age, annoyed at each small ache;
stumbled a little on the tennis court but dealt
that half-blind lethal serve, the way

old Chinese painters draw their single curve
of black on white, the brush a thousandth
time trailing its ink exact as grace,
the lifeline, mark of what's not self

but gesture, word, embrace: the way we are
in the world, as it's time to leave it.  In the eye
of the sun, one fast ball low across the net, and then
goodbye.

## My Parents in the Rose Garden

I lean on the ribbed wood sill
of the bathroom window, and look out
and down. Wisteria in green curls
comes indoors, pale trumpet blooms the scent
of this house, this time

and the two of them down there
walking on the bald lawn,
shadow already under the damson trees.
They walk a rectangle, hand in hand,
looking at roses.

They pause to look, talk, I see
him smile, she straightens
her spine to be up to it, to him,
to their continuing daily
stepping out.

Forever now, or for as long as I
shall live, I see them,
framed by green tendrils of
wisteria; among roses,
among the things of a lifetime
walking their bounds.

# WHO HAS SEEN OUR ORIGINAL FACE?

*for my children*

I, if anyone, should know.
Startled into air,
your first stare after birth, for me.

That first sharp glance
and afterwards, each time we met,
the recognition.
Is this love, could this stunned meeting
possibly become love?

I fought for you with feral guile;
we did our best;
you were staunch,
flexing in your boxed
solitudes.

In the absence
of ease, shut from
the warm room
of the normal,
we met in the open, finally
wide-eyed.

You came towards me
exhausted messengers
carrying clues I have still not
deciphered, telling me over and over
if I can listen

where you came from
and why.

## THE QUESTION

Who wanted me?
My son asks, blue gaze
over rimless glasses
all this time later

in the cafeteria
of a science museum
where past, present, future
are on separate floors

and a glass box hoists us
from Spitfires, sewing machines
and trams, through today's streets
and the Internet, towards

articulate robots,
genetic engineering and
new stars.

Knowing what you knew,
the risk and chance of prematurity
was it you or him?
Who chose, who staked the dare
to have another child?

Pizza-eating on the second floor,
that is, the present, I remember
my surprising hunger for him,
astonishment when he came out,

our boy, and the way both of us,
his father and I, sat in tears,

holding hands over tea cups
as I bled and they wheeled him

to the ICU, here and then
gone in a clatter of trolleys
to an incubator on the top floor.

Each of us, whatever
had gone on  before, wanting him more
each minute he was gone.

## MOTHER, DAUGHTER

A lace curtain dots its sprigs
upon a changing sky.

I could lie here
on my daughter's bed,
do nothing, watch
the play of the world's light,
tumbling clouds.

Between tea and dinner,
thinking of a drink
but not getting up yet; words
like sea glass smoothed and scumbled
in my head; just remembering,

letting it all flow through me,
time, the five o'clock of it,
lost stories, everything I ever
glimpsed or was set alight by.

Stones in a pocket, still
with their gleam on;
the endless fascinations.

## In The Borders

The swollen rivers of this country,
the wide Tweed, the Blackadder
run flush to the red earth;

between rowan and flaring elder
the dogs, Tess and Gemma, run
twined like bright ribbons,
snapping their young white teeth.

In our boots and waterproofs we go
plodding; as they weave their leaping
arcs, we raise eyes to the low sky:

light settles on a far field, a wall,
a slope of hill, grass shivers
like fur on a dog's back, the river
will rise in the night.

I am in my daughter's house.
She has made bread, jam, marmalade, yoghourt,
cake, she has painted these walls,

the child who watched me make bread, jam,
marmalade, yoghurt, cake, who saw herbs grow,
young trees set in earth, the holes dug square,
house plans sketched

upon note-pads and old envelopes, who was there
in the raw beginnings, ruined barns,
shared farmsteads, those rough attempts at home;

has made these decades later, her own version;
I sit in her kitchen, watch
rain at her windows, its straight fall.

## The Borderer

My old friend the poet claps a tweed hat
on his head, boots laced, his waxed coat fastened,
takes the dog's lead. My husband and I follow.
To the Peel tower, Scots pines, rocks,
the path uphill: the tea-brown Tweed.

He has written the poem
of his life, he was made to, death
gripped him in its terrier jaws, shook him,
set him down startled to begin again.

We three walk back in soft rain.
Past the good butcher, the cake shop,
the gents' outfitters that was,
the giddy memorial's surprise—
far too many young Borderers
chopped down in the Great War—
and home to tea and scones.

My old friend has a dog now
and a stone house with a view of hills
and the words which come after.

## Rain, Dorset

A day of rain,
digestive biscuits and tea-bags,
pillow-cases hung like wet flags
on the washing line.

A day of birds
fluffed out in the hedge
and the soaked heads
of blue hydrangeas
and nobody here but me

watching the rain, hoping
for poetry.  It all gets so tiny
as you watch for each
leaf-shake, twig-shift,
and the squirrel

who might just run
down the high wire
scattering big drops like mercury
as you make lunch.

It all gets to be just me
and this. Nobody comes,
there isn't even
a phone call

just wind, rain,
and the silence
that I can miss so
when it's always here,
when I'm not.

But I remember
that most of history was
like this: rain, wind,
birds in the hedge,
nobody coming, no words,
invasions only once or twice
in a thousand years

and that they
were glad of it.

IV.

## Burning Bowl

On New Year's Eve at midnight
we burned our hopes and wishes
in a metal bucket
under a full moon.

I knew then what must go:
certainty, the roof above us, the floor below,
plans and their outcomes,
constancy of weather.

I threw my folded scraps in, saw black paper
frill to ash in the blue fire.
Someone threw vodka on to make it burn
faster, bluer and more absolute.

Bread, a tablecloth, candles in the dark.
Paint on my friend's knuckle.
The clean glass, the straight flame.
The moon yellow behind the gumbo limbo.

This table laid in darkness, where we sit
talk, eat, drink, before we're
thrown to the burning bowl
of the coming year.

## Portuguese Man O' War

You know it
when you feel its nearly unbearable
touch, the electric tentacle
reaching through water you thought
clear, on a day you thought calm.
Bob of the poison sac merry
as a balloon, and you whipped,
drawn on, flounder through shallows
marked with its signature,
back to the safe land.
Pain works its flower
and bloom in you
and won't let up, you will walk
for days with its tattooed
necklaces upon your skin,
saying here it is, what waits
this spring in the heated seas
where too much nutrient
feeds these creatures till
they cluster and swarm,
here is the sign at last
of what hooks the heart
to bump unevenly, to tell us
in the flesh, what's wrong.

## FOR ERIK

They say cats know
when it's the last time they'll see you.

How you talked that night, and rubbed
the tabby's jaw, her throat, her belly,
flattened ears, elastic stripe of flank

after the Prosecco and the Thai fish
in coconut milk, as the moon
hooked your yard,

the season turning gently
towards fall, with Rachel Maddow
on TV, the cat's rough ecstasy

as you stroked, and all the time
a hole not yet dug in the red earth
of Africa;

and none of us knowing
but the cat knowing

my friend, your grave
in the opened earth of Africa
a tunnel of night away

and only your hand's movement
as the purring grew, to tell of it.

# The Blue Line, or
# What Does This Painting Know?

*Art Matters,* Peter de Bolla
*for J.M.M.*

It knows blue. It knows a fast vertical
trickle of paint from the wet brush.
It knows four beings in a row. It knows
gathering speed. Even vertigo.

She turns it right way up, I have been
looking at it in her kitchen,
my head on one side as if trying
to greet someone doing yoga.

She says, it is called *The Blue Line.*
The blue line is there, horizontal
now, and the people, they are people,
pass in their separate compartments

and she tells me, it is about
their suffering, their separation,
it is a train, passing. It is
*The Blue Line.* She has

tickets to paste on, to explain
but I'm waiting, not for the train
nor for its suffering occupants
whom I may recognize,

but for the painting.  For it
to speak and tell me what it knows
about the blue line and where
it leads and what pulls me

along behind it like someone
on a station platform who has to run
waving her handkerchief, maybe
in tears and certainly alone.

# The Writer's Brain

They took something out. Stitches
in the side of his head among the shaved hairs;
I thought of a cat I had, a small patch
marked only by neat sewing
and a little dried blood.

Funny, he said, how such a small thing
going in the brain…

Sixty years of wordplay, images,
deft as opponents up against the net,
batting meaning back and forth:
puns, poems, doubles entendres -

the brain soft as an apple in the grass.

I had trouble, he said, keeping
In touch with myself. I seemed
to have gone. But where?

They asked him questions
afterwards: What is your name?
Age? Date of birth?
Where do you think you are?
What is your profession?

Science professor, said the poet,

tired by then of realism,
and you can guess my age.
They weren't sure if they had him then,
or if he'd left for good.

# Eating Asparagus

I watch you knife them flat
upon the plate and scrape
their cooked green stalks apart

their fine urinal scent
already on the air
the butter running clear—

a kind of rape, it seems,
of this year's tender first—
as you separate, dissect, discard.

Shocked, I pick mine up whole,
dangle the glistening heads into my mouth
and hardly need to bite.

Since first as kids, we called them
"fried bluebells", delighted
in food we could eat with our fingers,

I've eaten them this way lifelong
without a thought.  Now
seeing you scalpel

gentle vegetable spears apart,
I wonder what next vast gap may well
appear between us.

# WRITING LIFE

When it comes, the answer is often
what you first thought of all those years ago,
the one you rejected.

Oh, the simplicity of it
that can't be arrived at simply
but only by a long road winding
through years and many metaphors
crossed out, and wanderings

down yellow pages, in black pen,
with phone numbers jotted
in their margins, and strange stains;

reached one late night when
you have almost given up hope
when failure stares out of the dark
and you think quite suddenly
oh, what the hell
and go there.

There. The place that was waiting
that you couldn't see; that longed
for you to give up cleverness
and guile, and just arrive.

## ON READING ANTOINE EMAZ

*"Bizarre sensation que cette odeur de
poireau tranché va me mener quelque
part ." (Cambouis)\**

He says, if you just go on cutting up the carrots
and leeks to make the evening's soup,
sooner or later the carrots and leeks—
such ordinary things yet with the sharp whiff
about them of the real—you will get there,
the quotidian will seep into the poem,
this sharp evanescent taste of the moment
sectioned on the chopping-board free
of the present and the past, will lie
under your hand, under the marked knife
on the board with its thousand crossways
cuts, it will leak out its essence
even if the smell of the leeks, that sharp
woody odor that was to remind you
of something, somewhere, fades;
as you can't remember what it was
you wanted to write, as you are
picked up and deposited, written
as it were into place—that place
you longed for, all along. The daily things
in their vegetable simplicity will make
the poem. Much like the soup, really,
if you can only let it simmer long enough.

\* *"Strange feeling that this smell of sliced leeks is going to take me
somewhere...." A. E.*

# Writing a Poem Every Morning

The way I brew coffee in a small Italian pot
and wait for its sudden breath
the way I watch milk rise in the pan
and use the same thick china cup,
set butter, orange marmalade, one knife
on the round table in the yard
to wait for toast and note the pink hibiscus
flowers' size and count the fallen mangoes
in the grass; see if the grass and herbs need
water and if it's a mockingbird or pigeon
that flies in—
Would it be the same each morning?
The same poem I mean,
like breakfast-making, teeth-cleaning,
coffee-sipping; or would it
find a life, no matter how I try
constricting it and fly up on that branch
to perch and sing, unrecognizable bird?

# This Painting Holds Your Absence.

*for Vogel, a Pantoum*

This painting holds your absence
I come in from the rough outdoors
Your hand thinner than I have ever seen it
Your spring yard, plumbago blue

I come in from the rough outdoors
I sense a change in you
Your spring yard, plumbago blue
Where are you bound, old friend?

I sense a change in you
Your blue flowers growing wildly forever
Where are you bound, old friend?
Your women have come to you

Your blue flowers growing wildly, forever
Wooden arms of the mango juggler
Your women have come to you
Have you guessed already?

Wooden arms of the mango juggler
So many mornings I've arrived here
Have you guessed already?
Your canvas wrapped in a sheet of today's paper

So many mornings I've arrived here
Your hand thinner than I have ever seen it
Your canvas wrapped in a sheet of today's paper
This painting holds your absence

## Poems Used To

Poems used to appear, fickle
as weather the forecast never predicted;
in the fast count between lightning flash
and thunder, I'd rush to scribble
what so precipitately came.

There wasn't a you in those poems,
they were before I'd even found a love object,
way before any idea of audience.
Just an I, silly as a hatless person in a downpour
solipsist on the page.

It was like getting a message by radar,
or on a bad phone line. No way
to order another, or dare a rewrite;
one-shot, its provenance unknown.

Now, it's a matter of small prosy wonderings:
a flower, a butterfly, the taste of espresso.
Today's sky. My teeth, or some other
body part I fear to lose. Now, I confess,
I need you, the reader, to be there,

tell me you get it, even
feel the same; life flowing past us,
no detail too small, banal or frail to matter.

# OYSTERS MUSCOVITE

*for C.B.*

They are so clean, their insides
transparent as new teeth.
Pearly might be the word,
though we can't find the right one
for the green caterpillar's romp
upon your jacket sleeve,
or the exact taste of the Californian
cabernet.

Black caviar, sour cream,
a drop of radish, lemon, then—
what? That rinse
that makes the palate itch,
soft bodies squashed between tongue
and roof.  Six is never quite enough
but  I pass one over,
wanting you not to miss this:
sharp, grit, clear, salt, ache.

We stare at each other, wordless.
We could say something about
the wine finally, or maybe tonight's
north wind out there among the masts
of Key West Bight;
but these oysters?

Naming the taste that's
almost seawater,
almost sex. Something
so evanescent that it's gone

as you think it. Salt of this
liquid world we're part of.
Bodies. Origins.

# DIANE ARBUS AT THE MET

It's hard, when you've followed a life
even for an hour, nose to the fading photos
somebody else took of her, the tiny
notebooks, scraps and exclamations,
to find: she killed herself.
Why? Wasn't this all enough?
There are clues: visits to a shrink,
the arbitrary storms of love, and
hanging out with the insane.
But the insane look so jolly, at their mad
parties with masks and little white socks,
their billowing nighties, like balloons
floating wrinkled to bounce gently
on the earth and up again.  It can't have been them,
those hook-nosed prancing dames and little
crouching friendly dwarfs in hotel rooms,
it can't, surely, have been anything
the lone transvestite said, or the stare
of the rich widow in her clutter
on Pennsylvania Avenue?  In here,
in the dark, I peer at the life, the bits
we all have, that may fail at any time;
while out there, beautifully framed,
hung, what she made of it all
stares back naked and unafraid.
Is it what we see that saves us?  While
inside, what we are in spite of it
struggles with the details, finds
one bleak morning suddenly not enough?

V.

# In Peru

All the Spanish I had learned
went out like the tide.
Just a croak of English longing
and the need to read.
One book in the hotel lobby:
Gabriel Garcia Marquez, in English,
his autobiography
to be taken in small doses,
made to last.


I drank Pisco Sours.
washed down aspirin, sent
for cough medicine.
Found someone
to inject me, blood
on the clinic floor, a syringe
to take away and use.
Coughed up the dirt of the city
of Lima, sweated in taxis, shivered
in the heat.


No, I did not see Cuzco, Macchu Picchu,
the gold of the Incas.
I was sitting on the toilet
when the earthquake came,
5.8 on the Richter,
imagined an old washer-dryer flung
into its spin cycle
on the floor below.
We stood under lintels to be safe.

Everyone was kind. The priest,
my brother, sister-in-law, three nieces
wearing their flowers for the wedding,
their nails done.
Their grandmother.
What can we do for you, they asked, what
do you need?

Air I can breathe. My husband.
China tea.  More than one book.
No mountains to go up.  Simplicity
of language. No decisions. Home.

## PILGRIMAGE

Buen Camino!
shout the Spanish cyclists
frog-thighs crammed into Lycra
as they splash up
high waterfalls

and the man who's walked from Germany
with his mule says only
"Es ist mein Tier."
The mule, poor Brother Ass,
doesn't say a thing.

The talk, when we have it,
is of feet. Stigmata
link us, blisters
ripped open at the Spanish
Red Cross in a high village

as the nurse strips plasters off
with skin, and we sing
Besame Mucho, loud
against the pain.

Compeed is bad, she says, we need
Betadine, and pure gauze.
The feet must breathe.

Feet, knees, sleep, rain.
Steep paths.  Five kilometers
before coffee.
A beer ahead like a promise.
Talk to me. Sing.
Tell me your life story.

A Canadian is mourning her mother.
A Scot is just up for the walk.
My answer is a blackbird
on a branch in the clean air
of Galicia after rain.

When we limp at last
into Santiago, fall
to the cold stone
of the cathedral floor
as the clock strikes
as the Venezuelan musicians play
under the arch
and the sun bangs its afternoon gong,

something shifts inside
like digestion.
Even the language, X-marked,
slides off the map
at the far western end
of Europe where
a saint's bones, they say,
washed up once

and a line forms
to hug his statue
and I know now, so much
doesn't matter, including this.

# THE FIRE CANOPY

*for K.K. and Larry*

I push the latch up and go in.
To my left, in the dark garden,
the fountain, water trickle, moss;
to my right, the fire.
Logs shift in the iron cage,
No one's here yet though
they will all soon come
bringing soup and the wine
and a book of poems,
and we will read into the night.
But now, offcuts of sculpture,
black olive, mahogany,
the Spanish lime felled
on the street, shiver together
in the torque of flame.
Trees once sliced open
live again where my friends have placed
their secret hearts on view.
Tonight the fire raises their ghosts
skyward, smoke to stars,
to heft their wide canopy
and cover us.

## Eclipse

Full moon — it has to be full
to eclipse, no half measures here,
but a cloudy night, the eye of it
slowly closed, its cataract
skin, earth shadow
pinkish, bruised
as when his eye grew
its curtain, those years ago.
I remember the drive
to Miami to save an eye
the slow veiling of it
after, the blur of his keen
glance.

I want the moon free now,
gold pod of our tropic,
swung clear of cloud
to sail its light across
the Atlantic, to cast
my own black shadow;
no uncertain ambiguous stare.
But look, you only have to doubt
for an hour, it's coming out
fine, the moon, and the eye
skimmed of its untimely
skin, saw better he said
than ever.

# LUNCH WITH L., GARRISON BIGHT

All the time we were talking
I watched the billow of red silk
she had pinned over the door,
how it filled, emptied
in the suck of wind

and behind it the glimmer
of water where after lunch
a tarpon fin turned
under the white knotted lines;

the water slopped between
houseboat and dock, we could feel
the floor shift gently and we said
how living on water reminds us
nothing is permanent.

We ate frittata and a salad
of small tomatoes and talked
of how love affairs begin simple
and then are not
and of how, on another day

we could be swept away
in a violent wave from here,
the whole frail boat she lives in
crushed to bits, everything
upended and incoming
as death, and only

the red silk membrane
left floating in the wreck

would tell how we sat here,
ate frittata, talked of art
and love affairs
the way people always have, and will.

# CHRISTMAS EVE, HIDDEN BEACH, KEY WEST

Last night the moon like a hammock,
a damp warm wind from the sea;

we stood on balconies and spoke
in two languages.

We talked of polar bears, the icecaps,
ate salmon from Alaska.

We greeted each other like family.
A new baby, black eyes reflecting light.

A man I have not seen for a year.
Embraces. We grow older,

we have grown a year older, and the man
in white linen remembers,

the woman at the table in the dark
of the yard, where the ocean

breathes and fumbles at our edges,
turns her hand up open to the air

to feel it a little longer, moving through.

## ASHES

Body, I trust you: what choice have I?
You go on while I do other things.
Write, cook dinner,
look at the sky.

I have spent my life
doing other things; while you get on
with it.
If you were to fail — and you will —
what is there to continue?

My friend's ashes blown out over the ocean
one dark evening made a ghost-shape
white against the incoming tide, and I,
I had her grit
under my fingernails.

We drank wine,
looked at the pictures on the screen;
the white wraith of her
continued over the wave.

That night,
thinned and beautiful, she came to us.
Everyone who was there
dreamed of her.
Which was she, ash or dream?

Who did I rinse from under my nails
in the restaurant washroom before dinner
that evening?

At the wake, we wept;
in our beds, dreamed.
A white shape flew out over the water
just as the osprey returned to her nest of sticks.

We felt, going our separate ways
after that dinner when she was on all our lips
that we had understood something.
Today, I can't tell you what.

Perhaps I am more substantial in my body;
perhaps a part of me flies out, white, over the water.

# THE DANCING PARTY

We danced to the edge
where the ocean cleaned
its shallows and the fire bugs flew,

we danced and others watched
under the Chinese lanterns
glowing like pomegranates;

a ship went out lit
and beautiful in the darkness

like a movie, everyone said,
like Fellini, a hulk of coarse
metal transformed by light.

It was an evening
for transformations,
he and I wordless
after quarrelling

holding each other under stars,
under lanterns, trusting
only the music and the dance,

and the night and the ocean
going on and on, the edge
of it all, and we

with our parts still half-
learned, our feet awkward

our dance another try,

with everyone there
loving each other awkwardly

dancing their strange dances,
everyone still alive.

# Florida Keys/Falluja

An old dog sleeps in the sun
eyes shut under the coconut.
Wind in the masts and stays.
a tick of halyards.

Someone talks on a cell phone;
the boats rise and fall like breath.
This morning, this Sunday morning,
we heard Falluja was taken.
A thousand dead; they called them all
insurgents.

Imagine a thousand people.
No, I can't imagine them alive
let alone dead.  Imagine ten people
standing here in the sun
like those three in ball caps and loose shirts.
Imagine women. Ten friends. Imagine
children, babies.  A dog.

Imagine the dog suddenly blown to pieces.
Imagine just one person,
who might have escaped had dawn come
a minute later, or earlier.

On this quiet Sunday, imagine:
the one person upon whom
life depends, the one you can't
imagine living without; yes, that one.
One is enough.

The vultures turn here,
wings transparent, slate-gray
at the tips, riding their thermals.
Over Falluja this morning, what hangs
in the sky?  What black bird
hovers, strong enough to clean the bones?

# Helmand Province/ Selly Oak

He's in a rented wheelchair
outside the pizza place
just round the corner from the hospital
our boys come back to, from Afghanistan.
His torn pant legs end, no knees or shins.
Eighteen maybe, eyes like harebells.

My son scoots in his own chair
to meet him; no combatant
in these wars, yet he knows the lifelong
score. Says, hi.

The boy says, *I lost my legs. In Helmand
Province. An antitank mine.
And my thumb.*

His mother from Glasgow at his side,
smiling, still numb.
*Eight weeks in the hospital, tomorrow
we're going home.*
She shows on her mobile phone
a photo, a bloody something, could be
a severed thumb.

*They made a new one,
look* — the blubbery thing,
stitch marks everywhere.
He says, *I saw my family, all of them,
when I was up in the air, Dad, Mum,
sister, granny, everyone.
Then I came down and saw my legs
a little way away. My thumb.*

We mothers look at each other.
My son is showing him his tattoos.
Tattoos are what you get to make up for everything.
*I'm getting the names of all my platoon*
*on my back. And when I get my new legs, ken,*
*I'm going straight back out.*

My son says, can I shake your hand?
From his own chair he shakes the good hand, the left.
He says, thank you for what you did.

The boy nods, a soldier's nod. He still has
the story of what happened, he can
tell it and tell it, it is all he has now,

and his dead friend, who saved him,
and the boys out there
and the way he was due to go
home, only the day after.

There's a ramp now up to the pizza place
that's near the hospital; it's why
we go there, all of us.
The boy and his mother move towards it
to sit across a table and not speak,

that look on them,
like people shouldering arms for a last haul.

## Poetry in Time of War

I want to forget their names, the generals,
advisors, puppet rulers,
the puffed-up and the brought-low,

I want not to know them,
not hear their plans, their excuses,
the President and the President's men,
the Pope with his white smoke for voodoo,

the suits, ties, teeth, insignia,
the guns, the names of trucks and weapons.

I want to forget them all,
to be washed of them,
to begin again: where no one knows who anyone is,
or what he believes.

To give my attention to:
frangipani leaves uncurling,
the smell of jasmine,
one person helping another across a street;

to the seeds,
to the beginnings; to one clear word for which
there is no disguise and no alternative.